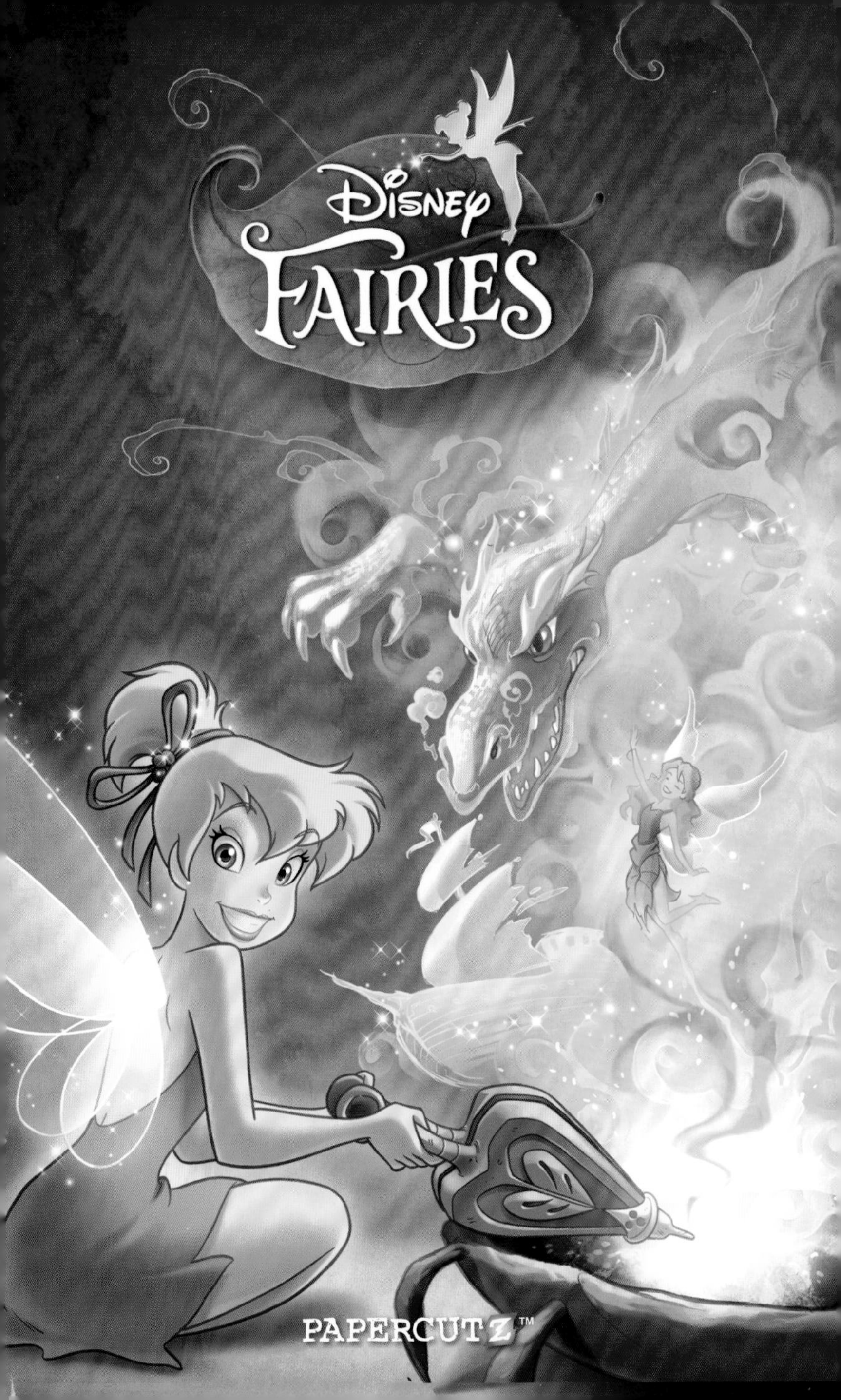
Disney
FAIRIES
PAPERCUTZ™

Graphic Novels Available from
PAPERCUTZ

Graphic Novel #1
"Prilla's Talent"

Graphic Novel #2
"Tinker Bell and the
Wings of Rani"

Graphic Novel #3
"Tinker Bell and the Day
of the Dragon"

Graphic Novel #4
"Tinker Bell
to the Rescue"

Graphic Novel #5
"Tinker Bell and
the Pirate Adventure"

Graphic Novel #6
"A Present
for Tinker Bell"

Graphic Novel #7
"Tinker Bell the
Perfect Fairy"

Graphic Novel #8
"Tinker Bell and her
Stories for a Rainy Day"

Graphic Novel #9
"Tinker Bell and
her Magical Arrival"

Graphic Novel #10
"Tinker Bell and
the Lucky Rainbow"

Graphic Novel #11
"Tinker Bell and the
Most Precious Gift"

Graphic Novel #12
"Tinker Bell and the
Lost Treasure"

Graphic Novel #13
"Tinker Bell and the
Pixie Hollow Games"

Graphic Novel #14
"Tinker Bell and Blaze"

**Tinker Bell and the
Great Fairy Rescue**

COMING SOON

Graphic Novel #15
"Tinker Bell and the
Secret of the Wings"

DISNEY
FAIRIES

#3 "Tinker Bell and the
Day of the Dragon"

Contents

The Cobweb   5

The Fox and the Fairies   18

Fairy Riddles   31

Talents After a Fashion   44

Day of the Dragon   57

PAPERCUTZ™

NEW YORK

"The Cobweb"
Script: Teresa Radice
Revised Dialogue: Stefan Petrucha
Layout: Elisabetta Melaranci
Pencils: Andrea Greppi
Inks: Marina Baggio
Color: Litomilano

"The Fox and the Fairies"
Script: Giulia Conti
Revised Dialogue: Stefan Petrucha
Layout: Emilio Urbano
Pencils: Manuela Razzi
Inks: Marina Baggio
Color: Litomilano
Page 18 Art:
Pencils: Manuela Razzi and Emilio Urbano
Inks: Roberta Zanotta
Color: Andrea Cagol

"Fairy Riddles"
Script: Augusto Machetto
Revised Dialogue: Stefan Petrucha
Layout and Pencils: Elisabetta Melaranci
Inks: Marina Baggio
Color: Stefania Santi
Page 31 Art:
Pencils: Bruno Enna
Inks: Elisabetta Melaranci
Color: Andrea Cagol

"Talents After a Fashion"
Script: Carlotta Quattrocolo
Revised Dialogue: Stefan Petrucha
Layout and Pencils: Elisabetta Melaranci
Inks: Marina Baggio
Color: Stefania Santi
Page 44 Art:
Pencils and Inks: Elisabetta Melaranci
Color: Andrea Cagol

"Day of the Dragon"
Script: Augusto Machetto
Revised Dialogue: Stefan Petrucha
Layout: Elisabetta Melaranci
Pencils: Cristina Giorilli
Inks: Marina Baggio
Color: Litomilano
Page 57 Art:
Pencils: Andrea Greppi
and Emilio Urbano
Inks: Marina Baggio
Colors: Andrea Cagol

Chris Nelson and Caitlin Hinrichs – Production
Beth Scorzato – Production Coordinator
Michael Petranek – Associate Editor
Jim Salicrup – Editor-in-Chief

ISBN: 978-1-59707-128-4 paperback edition
ISBN: 978-1-59707-129-1 hardcover edition

Printed in China
May 2014 by Asia One Printing, LTD
13/F Asia One Tower
8 Fung Yip St., Chaiwan, Hong Kong

Papercutz books maye be purchased for business or promtional use.
For information on bulk purchases please contact Macmillan Corporate and Premium
Sales Department at (800) 221-7945 x5442

Distributed by Macmillan.

Second Papercutz Printing

IT'S THAT TIME OF YEAR WHEN PIXIE HOLLOW BUSTLES WITH ACTIVITY IN PREPARATION FOR QUEEN CLARION'S ARRIVAL DAY!

THE COBWEB

FOR ON THAT DAY, EACH FAIRY GIVES THE QUEEN A SPECIAL GIFT...

...BASED ON HER OWN *TALENT!*

SO, PRILLA, WHAT ARE *YOU* GOING TO GIVE THE QUEEN?

SINCE I'M LUCKY ENOUGH TO BE AN *HONORARY MEMBER* OF ALL THE TALENT GROUPS, I WANT TO TAKE ADVANTAGE OF THAT...

"...AND JOIN QUEEN CLARION'S *HELPER FAIRIES!*"

GLAD TO HAVE YOU, PRILLA!

WAIT UNTIL THE QUEEN SEES WHAT A *SPECIAL* JOB WE'LL DO ON THIS ROOM!

IT'LL BE GREAT!

BUT IT ALREADY *IS* GREAT! THE WALLS ARE ENCHANTING... THE FLOOR, AMAZING! NOT TO MENTION THE BED!

BACK IN PIXIE HOLLOW, A FRIEND'S HEART FILLS WITH CONCERN...

IT'S DARK AND THE QUEEN'S PARTY IS READY TO START!

BUT PRILLA, FIRA, AND BECK AREN'T BACK! I HEARD THEY WERE LOOKING FOR A GIFT, BUT THEY'RE SO LATE!

I SHOULD *TELL* SOMEBODY...

BACK IN THE FOREST, THINGS ARE DARK, BUT NO LONGER SO DANGEROUS.

AW! THE SPIDER'S AFRAID OF US! HE'S A PRISONER, TOO! I FEEL IT!

HUH? HOW'S A SPIDER GET CAUGHT IN ITS OWN WEB?

YEAH, BECK, HOW?

"OH, HE WAS PROBABLY SPINNING HIS *FIRST* WEB, AND NOT BEING AN EXPERT..."

ALL IT TOOK WAS A GUST OF WIND TO...WRAP THINGS UP ON THE POOR GUY!

WE CAN'T JUST LEAVE HIM OR *YOU* UP THERE!

PRILLA, YOU *SPECIALIZE IN RIPS*, DON'T YOU?

THE FOX AND THE FAIRIES

- 20 -

SPLASH

SNIFF SNIFF

YOU MEAN OL' FOX! *MY WINGS ARE SOAKED!* HOW CAN I FLY NOW?

HE CAN'T UNDERSTAND YOU! HE'S A FOX AND YOU'RE NOT AN ANIMAL-TALENT FAIRY!

I KNOW! COME ON, LET'S HIDE IN THAT OLD LOG!

YELLING JUST MADE ME FEEL BETTER! NOT AS GOOD AS SEEING *YOU* THOUGH! THANKS FOR SAVING MY LIFE!

WE'RE NOT SAVED YET! THANK ME LATER!

FANTASTIC! HE'LL BE HAPPY ON THE OTHER SIDE OF THE RIVER, AND WE'LL ALL BE SAFE!

THAT WAS SO BRAVE, TERENCE! AND STRONG! AND...

YOU SAVED US!

CLAP CLAP

AND *YOU* SAVED ME!

AND *YOU* SAVED ME!

PHOOEY! I HATE HUGGING AS MUCH AS I HATE FAIRY FREEZE TAG!

BUT IN HER HEART EVEN VIDIA KNOWS FAIRY DUST ISN'T THE *ONLY* KIND OF MAGIC! THERE'S ALSO...

...COOPERATION!

THE END

FAIRY RIDDLES

ATTENTION ALL FAIRIES! OUR DEAR PRILLA'S HAD A WONDERFUL IDEA!

WE'RE GOING TO HAVE A SPECIAL *TREASURE HUNT!*

FANTASTIC! I'M UP FOR THAT! HOW ABOUT YOU, *DULCIE?*

SOUNDS SWEET AS A COOKIE!

IT'S SPECIAL BECAUSE IT'S ALSO A *RIDDLE* CONTEST! THE RIDDLE WILL TELL YOU WHAT TREASURE TO BRING BACK!

AH-HAH! SO WE'LL *ALSO* BE HUNTING FOR ANSWERS!

THE RIDDLES WE USE SHALL BE FROM THE BIG BOOK OF FAIRIES!

WOW! THAT'S WHERE WE FAIRIES HAVE *ALWAYS* KEPT *ALL OUR SECRETS!*

YES! FOREVER AND EVER! IT'S GOT ADVICE, CURIOSITIES, FACTS, LEGENDS, PROVERBS, COOKING TIPS...

AND RULES ABOUT *INTERRUPTING!* MAY I CONTINUE, *BECK?*

OOPS! I'D FLY BACKWARD, QUEEN CLARION...

TO BEGIN, I'LL READ THREE RIDDLES! RIDDLE ONE: "IT'S LIKE RAIN, BUT IT'S HARD. AND IF I CATCH IT... IT DISAPPEARS!"

"IT'S ROUND, BUT DOESN'T ROLL. VIOLET, BUT HAS NO PETALS!"

AND LAST BUT NOT LEAST: "IT FLIES, THEN IT DOZES, TASTES GREAT AND HAS THE COLOR OF THE SUN!"

IT'S SUPPOSED TO BE HARD! *SNOW* IS SOFT, REMEMBER?

THAT'S RIGHT! I SAW A PICTURE OF IT IN THE BIG BOOK ONCE...

ICE IS HARD, THOUGH, RIGHT? HOW ABOUT THE ICE-COLD CAVES! THEY SAY THERE'S ALWAYS *ICE* IN THERE!

AND THE ICE COMES FROM *RAIN!* NICE! GLAD I THOUGHT OF IT!

BUT RANI REMEMBERS THAT THE BIG BOOK IS FULL OF CREEPY LEGENDS ABOUT THE ICE-COLD CAVES...

THEY'RE COLD! AND DARK! AND... AND...NO ONE I KNOW HAS EVER GONE INSIDE...

BETTER YET! THAT MEANS I'LL BE THE FIRST!

NOT TO WORRY! IF ANYTHING IS IN THERE, IT *CAN'T* BE AS FAST AS I AM! BACK IN A *FLASH!*

BRRR! IT *IS* COLD...

AND DARK! GUESS THE CRYBABY WAS RIGHT...

BUT WHAT'S THAT SHINING DOWN THERE? IT LOOKS LIKE *EYES*, BUT THERE ARE SO *MANY!*

HA! EYES MY FOOT! IT'S JUST A REFLECTION...

ON SOME *ICE!* ONE POINT, VIDIA; EVERYONE ELSE, *NOTHING!* HA!

CLUTCHING THE ICE, VIDIA POURS ON THE SPEED.

HEY! LOWER THOSE WINGS! WE HAVE TO *WALK* BACK TOGETHER!

DIDN'T YOU HEAR ME? THAT'S NOT *YOUR* TREASURE!

OH? THEN HOW DID I WIND UP *HOLDING* IT?

- 42 -

THE END

SOON IT'S TIME FOR THE **TRY-ON** SESSIONS...

SO, WHERE IS IT? SHOW ME PLEASE! I CAN'T WAIT!

FIRA! RANI! YOU LOOK **FABULOUS!**

THANKS! THESE DRESSES TAKE INSPIRATION FROM OUR TALENTS...

...LIGHT FOR FIRA AND WATER FOR ME!

AND ME? WHAT ABOUT ME? CAN I SEE MY **DRESS?** PLEASE, PLEASE, PLEASE?

UMM... WELL...

GEE... WE...

...HAD SOME... **PROBLEMS...**

- 50 -

- 51 -

BUT EVEN IF *PRILLA* SAYS SHE'S SATISFIED, HER FRIENDS ARE *NOT!*

WE'VE GOT TO COME UP WITH A *SOLUTION!*

OR AT LEAST A BETTER *DRESS!*

PRILLA, SIT WITH US! THE SCOUTING-TALENT FAIRIES' TABLE MISSES ITS *HONORARY* FAIRY!

IT'S BEEN DAYS SINCE YOU WERE AT THE MINING-TALENT FAIRIES' TABLE! FLY OVER HERE THIS INSTANT!

HOW CAN YOU TURN YOUR WINGS ON THE FAIRY-DUST-TALENT FAIRIES?

OH, YOU! YOU'RE ALL *EMBARRASSING* ME!

I'VE GOT IT*!!* LEAVE IT TO A TINKER-TALENT FAIRY TO *FIX* THINGS!

TINKER BELL, WHAT ARE YOUR WINGS FLUTTERING ABOUT NOW?

THAT EVENING, JUST BEFORE THE BIG PARTY...

÷SIGH!÷ WHAT BOTHERS ME MOST IS NOT BEING ABLE TO *EXPLAIN* MY TALENT!

YOU DON'T HAVE TO! WE ALL KNOW HOW *IMPORTANT* IT IS AND HOW *UNIQUE* YOU ARE!!

IT'S THANKS TO *YOUR* TALENT THAT THE CLUMSIES SEE *YOU* AND *BELIEVE* IN US!

OH, FIRA...

...THANK YOU SO, SO...!

...WHAT? WHAT IS *THAT*?

A BUBBLE-MESSAGE FROM RANI, FOR YOU! TOUCH IT!

PRILLA, FLY TO THE SEWING-TALENT WORKSHOP *RIGHT AWAY!* IT'S *URGENT!*

POP

YOU'RE FINALLY HERE!

...WE COULDN'T WAIT A *SECOND* LONGER!

WAIT? FOR WHAT?

IT TOOK A *THOUSAND* WING FLAPS TO THINK THIS UP!

BUT IN THE END, TINKER BELL HAD A *BRIGHT* IDEA!

IT WAS *OBVIOUS!* AFTER ALL, YOU'RE THE HONORARY FAIRY OF *ALL TALENTS!*

YES, I KNOW. AND...?

SO FOR YOUR DRESS, WE DECIDED *NOT* TO TAKE INSPIRATION FROM A SINGLE TALENT...

...BUT FROM *ALL* OF THEM!

FRUSH

- 54 -

DAY OF THE DRAGON

IN PIXIE HOLLOW EVERYONE WORKS TOGETHER, WITH EVERY FAIRY PLAYING THEIR PART.

GARDEN-TALENT FAIRIES KEEP THE FLOWERS LUSH AND BEAUTIFUL.

GET THOSE PETALS WATERED, GIRLS! THE SUN'S WORKING OVERTIME, SO *WE* SHOULD TOO!

WHILE POLISHING-TALENT FAIRIES BRING A SPARKLE TO THE DAY.

SHINE THOSE DOORKNOBS! EVERY *DROP* OF SUNLIGHT SHOULD BE REFLECTED!

BEAUTIFUL DAY, *QUEEN CLARION!*

IT CERTAINLY IS! AND HOW *LUCKY* WE ARE TO *HELP!*

HMM...BUT UNLESS THERE'S A LOT MORE DUST SOON, I WON'T BE DOING IT FOR VERY LONG!

THE MILL WAS WORKING ALL NIGHT... BUT THERE'S BARELY *HALF* OF WHAT THERE SHOULD BE!

GRIND
GRIND
GRIND
GRIND
CRUNCH
CRUNCH

WELL, *THAT* DOESN'T SOUND GOOD.

- 65 -

- 71 -

Discover the stories of
Tinker Bell and her fairy friends!

Prilla and the Butterfly Lie

Queen Clarion's Secret

The Trouble with Tink

© Disney Enterprises, Inc.

COLLECT THEM ALL!
Available wherever
books are sold.
Also available on audio.

WATCH OUT FOR PAPERCUTZ

Welcome, friends, to the third phantasmagorical DISNEY FAIRIES graphic novel from Papercutz. I'm Jim Salicrup, the Editor-in-Chief and one of those folks the fairies in Pixie Hollow call "clumsies." I'm here to talk to you about DISNEY FAIRIES and Papercutz—to tell you about everything that's new and exciting. Well, the news is so stupendous, so sensational, I can barely contain myself, so I better get right to it...

If you enjoyed the DISNEY FAIRIES DVDs, "Tinker Bell" and "Tinker Bell and the Lost Treasure," as much as I did, then you're going to be thrilled to find out that the third DISNEY FAIRIES DVD is in stores now! Yes, "Tinker Bell and the Great Fairy Rescue" is out now, and it's just as much fun as the first two were! Now, some of you may be wondering why I'm mentioning that here in the DISNEY FAIRIES graphic novel. I'll tell you why—because not only is "Tinker Bell and the Great Fairy Rescue" available as a DVD, it's also a graphic novel available from Papercutz!

As a comics editor, I'm also a comics fan and a comics collector. I'm even on the board of the Museum of Comic and Cartoon Art (www.moccany.org) in New York City because I love comics so much. And one of my favorite comics is the comicbook adaptation of PETER PAN originally published in 1952. That's where Tinker Bell made her comicbook debut! As wonderful as the original movie is—with such incredible animation, perfect voice acting, and unforgettable songs— there's a certain charm about having the same story in a comicbook that's indescribably special. That's why I'm so excited that Papercutz will be publishing "Tinker Bell and the Great Fairy Rescue" as a graphic novel.

And what a graphic novel it is! "Tinker Bell and the Great Fairy Rescue" is published at a bigger size than the DISNEY FAIRIES graphic novels—it's a big nine inches tall and a dainty six inches wide. And every comics page is devoted to telling "Tinker Bell and the Great Fairy Rescue"—it's a story so big and magical it fills up the entire graphic novel. We're so excited about this that on the following pages we're providing a very special preview of "Tinker Bell and the Great Fairy Rescue," but keep in mind that the actual graphic novel will be bigger, bolder, and brighter than the pages presented here. We just wanted to give you a little idea of what we're talking about.

There's just enough room to remind you that we want to know what you think of the DISNEY FAIRIES graphic novels. Email me at salicrup@papercutz.com or send a letter to us at: Disney Fairies, PAPERCUTZ, 40 Exchange Place, Suite 1308, New York, NY 10005. Also, be sure to visit www.disneyfairies.com for all the latest news direct from Pixie Hollow. And whatever you do, don't forget about the next DISNEY FAIRIES graphic novel! You'll get to see the encounter we're all eagerly waiting for—Vidia meets Captain Hook! It's in DISNEY FAIRIES #4 "Tinker Bell to the Rescue"!

Until then, this is Jim the honorary sparrow man wishing you Faith, Trust—and Pixie Dust!

JiM

WHEN SUMMER COMES, THE FAIRIES RIDE THE BREEZES TO THE *MAINLAND*. THAT'S WHERE THE *CLUMSIES* (WHICH IS WHAT THEY CALL PEOPLE LIKE YOU AND ME) LIVE!

SO MUCH TO DO AND SO MANY FAIRIES, EACH WITH A TALENT TO HELP REAWAKEN THE *SEASON*.

LIKE *WATER* FAIRY SILVERMIST, WHO MAKES SURE THE PONDS ARE CRYSTAL CLEAR...

GARDEN FAIRY ROSETTA, WHO HELPS THE FLOWERS STRETCH AND BLOOM...

LIGHT FAIRY IRIDESSA, WHO PUTS A SPARKLE ON THE SUNFLOWERS...

AND *ANIMAL* FAIRY, FAWN, WHO TEACHES BABY BIRDS TO FLY!

EVERY SUMMER, IT'S THE SAME, BUT FOR SOME, SUCH AS *TINKER BELL*, IT'S THE *FIRST* TIME.

HEY, *TINK!* READY FOR YOUR FIRST SUMMER ON THE MAINLAND?

ABSOLUTELY! IT'S SO BEAUTIFUL OUT HERE, *TERENCE!*

THERE IT IS, TINK! *FAIRY CAMP!*

HI, GUYS!

EVERY SUMMER, WHEN THEY ARRIVE, THE FAIRIES AND SPARROW MEN, LIKE *CLANK* AND *BOBBLE*, ALL SET UP A BASE.

IT'S EASIER TO WORK IN THE COOL AND QUIET BENEATH THE LEAVES, AWAY FROM *PRYING* EYES.

FAIRY CAMP ISN'T OUT IN THE OPEN... WE NEED TO STAY *HIDDEN* FROM HUMANS!

WE DO?

ER... NEED ANY HELP WITH THAT WAGON?

NOPE! SHE'S RUNNING FINE...

TINK, A TINKER-TALENT FAIRY, IS USUALLY *PLEASED* TO SEE HER INVENTIONS WORKING PROPERLY...

OKAY, GLAD TO HEAR IT!

BUT NOW IT LEAVES HER WITH *NOTHING* TO DO!

I *NEED* TO TINKER!

WHOA, YOU JUST GOT HERE! TAKE IT EASY!

HERE'S YOUR SUPPLY! I'VE GOT TO DELIVER PIXIE DUST TO OTHER FAIRY CAMPS...

AND DON'T WORRY! YOU'LL FIND SOMETHING TO FIX!

I *HOPE* SO...

Don't miss "Tinker Bell and the Great Fairy Rescue" Graphic Novel –
available at booksellers everywhere!